Days out in Autumn

Vic Parker

Heinemann
LIBRARY

Little Nippers

www.heinemann.co.uk/library
Visit our website to find out more information about **Heinemann Library** books.

To order:
☎ Phone 44 (0) 1865 888066
🖹 Send a fax to 44 (0) 1865 314091
🖳 Visit the Heinemann Bookshop at www.heinemann.co.uk/library to browse our catalogue and order online.

First published in Great Britain by Heinemann Library, Halley Court, Jordan Hill, Oxford OX2 8EJ, part of Harcourt Education. Heinemann is a registered trademark of Harcourt Education Ltd.

Editorial: Jilly Attwood and Claire Throp
Design: Jo Hinton-Malivoire and bigtop, Bicester, UK
Models made by: Jo Brooker
Picture Research: Rosie Garai, Sally Smith and Debra Weatherley
Production: Séverine Ribierre

Originated by Dot Gradations
Printed and bound in China by South China Printing Company

ISBN 0 431 17303 6 (hardback)
08 07 06 05 04
10 9 8 7 6 5 4 3 2 1

ISBN 0 431 17308 7 (paperback)
08 07 06 05 04
10 9 8 7 6 5 4 3 2 1

British Library Cataloguing in Publication Data
Parker, Vic
Days out in autumn
508.2
A full catalogue record for this book is available from the British Library.

Acknowledgements
The publisher would like to thank the following for permission to reproduce photographs: Alamy/Leslie Garland Picture Library p. **10–11**; Collections p. **18** (Nigel Hawkins); Corbis pp. **17 top**, 17 bottom, **15**, **19**; Gareth Boden pp. **20**, **21**; Getty Images p. **22–23** (Pauline Cutler); Reflections p. **12** (Jennie Woodcock); Robert Harding Picture Library p. **4** (Andy Williams), **16** (Jeremy Bright), p. **6**; Robert Harding p. **14** (N. Penny); Trevor Clifford pp. **5**, **7**, **8**, **9**, **13**.

Cover photograph reproduced with permission of Alamy/John Foxx.

The publishers would like to thank Annie Davy for her assistance in the preparation of this book.

Every effort has been made to contact copyright holders of any material reproduced in this book. Any omissions will be rectified in subsequent printings if notice is given to the publishers.

The paper used to print this book comes from sustainable resources.

Contents

It's autumn!

In autumn the leaves on many trees turn red and orange and brown.

Brrr! Autumn is chilly.

What should you wear to go out?

I spy in the park

In the park the leaves make a colourful carpet.

What else has fallen
from the trees?

Autumn art

You can make bright autumn pictures with leafprints.

Finished!

Let's go fly a kite

Autumn winds are good for flying kites.

What shapes can you see in the sky?

Blackberrying trip

Let's pick ripe blackberries from the hedgerow.

Mmm!

Blackberry pie for pudding! Yum!

It's Halloween!

It's fun to dress up in **scary**, spooky costumes for a Halloween party.

Beachcombing

Cold days on the beach are good for treasure hunts.

Can you find smooth pebbles or a pretty shell?

At the fun park

choo!
choo!

At a fun park, there are lots of exciting rides to try.

giddy up!

19

Helping in the garden

It's time to plant bulbs in the garden.

They will grow into spring flowers.

There is lots of tidying
up to do too!

It's bonfire night

pop!

bang!

fizz!

Index

The end

Notes for adults

The *Days out in…* series helps young children become familiar with the way their environment changes through the year. The books explore the natural world in each season and how this affects community life and social activities. Used together, the books will enable discussion about similarities and differences between the seasons, how the natural world follows a cyclical pattern, and how different people mark special dates in the year. The following Early Learning Goals are relevant to this series:

Knowledge and understanding of the world
Early learning goals for exploration and investigation
• look closely at similarities, differences, patterns and change.
Early learning goals for sense of time
• observe changes in the environment, for example through the seasons.
Early learning goals for cultures and beliefs
• begin to know about their own cultures and beliefs and those of other people.

This book introduces the reader to the season of autumn. It will encourage young children to think about autumn weather, wildlife and landscape; activities they can enjoy in autumn; and what clothes it is appropriate to wear. The book will help children extend their vocabulary, as they will hear new words such as *hedgerow* and *bulb*. You may like to introduce and explain other new words yourself, such as *wheelbarrow* and *sparkler*.

Additional information about the seasons

Not all places in the world have four seasons. Climate is affected by two factors: 1) how near a place is to the Equator (hence how much heat it receives from the Sun), 2) how high a place is (mountains are cooler than nearby lowlands). This is why some parts of the world have just two seasons, such as the hot wet season and the hot dry season across much of India. Other parts of the world have just one season, such as the year-long heat of the Sahara desert or the year-long cold of the North Pole.

Follow-up activities

• Make a collection of things you might find on an autumn beach walk: a feather, a bit of driftwood, a smooth pebble, a pretty shell, etc.
• Take a trip to a library to find out more about Halloween and the autumn festivals of other cultures.
• Make a pumpkin lantern for Halloween.